The Color of Gratitude

The Color of Gratitude

And Other Spiritual Surprises

ROBERT MORNEAU

ORBIS BOOKS

Maryknoll. New York 10545

Founded in 1970, Orbis Books endeavors to publish works that enlighten the mind, nourish the spirit, and challenge the conscience. The publishing arm of the Maryknoll Fathers and Brothers, Orbis seeks to explore the global dimensions of the Christian faith and mission, to invite dialogue with diverse cultures and religious traditions, and to serve the cause of reconciliation and peace. The books published reflect the views of their authors and do not represent the official position of the Maryknoll Society. To learn more about Maryknoll and Orbis Books, please visit our website at www.maryknollsociety.org.

Photo editor: Catherine Costello

Manufactured in the United States of America.

Library of Congress Cataloging-in-Publication Data

Morneau, Robert F., 1938-
  The color of gratitude : and other spiritual surprises / Robert Morneau.
     p. cm.
  ISBN 978-1-57075-846-1 (pbk.)
  I. Title.
  PS3563.O871936C65 2009
  811'.54--dc22

                              2009008958

Contents

Preface

It was the priest-poet Gerard Manley Hopkins (1844-1889) who captured so well an attitude that might might deepen our sensitivity and govern our lives: "There lives the dearest freshness deep down things" ("God's Grandeur"). In writing this, Hopkins was also keenly aware that there is much darkness and cruelty in human history. Earlier in the sonnet he describes how, down the generations, we have "seared" and "smeared" God's creation.

And yet, there is a great "freshness" that awaits us if our eyes are open, our ears are alert. We do live in a "divine milieu," for God's light, love, and life permeate our days and our hearts. Our challenge is to perceive and respond to the presence of grace.

Over the years I have attempted to be attentive. This is no easy task in a busy, noisy, and hurried world. For me, one means for slowing down and striving to practice a contemplative attitude is through writing. Pausing each morning, I reflect upon the previous day and watch for moments of "freshness," experiences that expand and refine the heart. Recently, this practice led to this poem:

A Splash of Sunshine

Each day I seek a sunbeam,
a luminous moment of grace,
be it a poetic passage,
a compassionate glance,

an affirmative word.
Just a single sunbeam,
nothing more.
This morning while walking,
a splash of sunshine
fell upon a maple tree.
It was too much,
like the Mount Tabor epiphany,
and I turned away overwhelmed.
I walked on
asking God to turn down His glory
lest I, like Milton,
too soon would lose my sight.

This volume is an invitation to take a walk in the woods, to sit
at table in leisurely conversation, to listen to a fellow pilgrim
seeking a sunbeam of God's grace. Who knows, it may even-
tually lead to a consistent realization that "there lives the
dearest freshness deep down things."

Bird Dog

Have you ever seen a bird dog
dashing across a meadow
suddenly freeze,
head erect,
front right paw off the floor of the earth,
tail extended,
ears pointing to the heavens?
Here is "frozen music" at its best,
better than any architectural feat.
Then, with the nod of the head,
the hunter releases from obedience the pointer,
the bird, now flushed,
ascends towards the sky and suddenly falls to earth.

Would that our soul
had the bird dog's instincts.
Would that we might sense
hidden truth and concealed love,
freeze for a moment and then
pursue these blessings with utmost speed.
Would that we might point Him out
in all the meadows of our lives.

I Need . . .

I need to walk the farm.
I need to feel the firm earth
and hear the call of birds
and smell the distant clover.
I need again to be one with nature,
even in her indifference.
Too long I've been among men and women,
and they with me.
I need the silence of open spaces
and the blueness of a lovely sky.
I need a piece of solitude
lest I die.

Waiting

My right toe was tapping,
my left thumb twitching
as I stood before the washing machine.
The wash and rinse cycle had done their duty,
and the "spin" turn was on stage,
on stage, on stage.
While standing and waiting
I came to know the meaning of Eternity.
Around and around the clothes spun
while I stood like a statue waiting, waiting, waiting.
Finally the click came,
the cylinder halted quickly.

Now I'm standing before the dryer,
as the laundry goes around and around and around
and I, I experience Eternity once more.

Time to Kill

Is murder a part of your history,
murder as in the killing of time?
Yesterday I had four hours
between scheduled events.
Time to kill, our culture calls it.
I refused the murder.
I took the time with me to a park,
watched the snow melting,
kids riding bikes on the ice,
lovers embracing,
a father and son hiking hand in hand.
I listened to the seagulls sing of spring,
felt the south wind wild my hair,
pondered large, melancholic questions.
It was time well spent, respected.
It was time bordering on eternity
and it offered a brief piece of peace.

Labyrinth

While jogging in the freshness of the morning,
running the perimeter of the retreat grounds,
I came upon a sign: "Labyrinth to the North."
I took the sign and jogged north
and there in the middle of the meadow
lay the circular maze.
Not wanting to break my running rhythm
I did the labyrinth in less than fifty-five seconds.

I think I missed the point—
the point of the labyrinth, the point of life.
Hurrying from here to there,
unaware of deeper, far-off things,
means that life passes us by—
or we pass it by.

When life is so missed,
a melancholy descends,
bringing, at the end of the run,
not euphoria but a sadness all too deep.

Eulogy

She changed the world.

Though orphaned early,
and knowing the Depression's poverty,
she became strong and independent,
wise and compassionate.

She changed the world.

Gave life to five children,
loved her husband for fifty-four years,
cherished her sixteen grandchildren,
put first things first.

She changed the world.

Nursing people back to health,
working and playing with gusto,
embracing God's will with a lively faith.

The world was changed
by one woman who loved
    her husband,
      her family,
        her God.

Cruise-Control Advice

The advice came from Texas,
the Lone Star State,
not known for abundant snow,
ice storms quite sporadic:
"Shut off the cruise-control
when driving in snow, on ice."
Wisconsin-born I already had this knowledge.
In inclement weather, don't give control to technology.

And life's journey?
Existence on cruise-control
works fine when all is well.
But on dark days, shut it off
and take each overpass and curve with care.

Pain

Leaves, as the fire nears,
curl in upon themselves—and are gone.

When suffering circles the human heart
it too folds inward,
drawn there by instinct, for self-protection.
The Spanish proverb got it right
about the world ending at the foot of one's sickbed.

Is there a way out, an alternative response?
Is fire consuming or transforming?
Is suffering destructive or redemptive?
Need the sickbed narrow our world to nothing but self?

When grace is at hand,
a trust in God's redeeming love,
even darkness holds light
and suffering, a hidden joy.
The gift of faith here—sheer grace!

The War

It was a distant war,
thousands of miles from our homeland,
a long, long way from the heart.
But yesterday the war drew near.
A young soldier,
from a neighboring village,
was killed in a helicopter crash.
The battle now had a face
and the moans of a grieving family.

No war is distant
though miles silence the sound of weapons.
We are one family, and
every war wears the face of
grieving humanity.

Tell Me

Tell me of your life, my soul,
not what you have read,
not the chapters of history,
not other people's experience,
but your own.
Too often you are a parrot,
telling me you want a cracker
when you really want love.
Too often your thoughts and feelings
are all vicarious,
arising from others' songs and speeches.
Tell me of your dreams,
your fears, your joys.
Do not go to the grave
with nothing of your own to bury,
with nothing of your own in which to glory.

Peekaboo

It's a glance, they say,
between babies and grownups.
I say it's life itself—
seeing and being seen.
In a glance,
the meeting of eyes,
all can be transformed.
Just ask Peter—
seen across an evening fire.
Just ask Mary—
standing beneath the Cross.

Candle and Music

I held in hand a candle,
the only light in the night's darkness.
I listened to a harpist play "Shenandoah,"
the only sound in the evening's stillness.
A candle and a song,
a light and a melody,
what more do we need?

A voice whispered: "Love."
We need a loving gaze
so that when the candle is extinguished
and the music is ended,
we are still not alone.

A candle,
a song,
a glance of love.

They Danced

They danced,
not a slow, meditative waltz
but a fast-stepping jig
that invited the audience to clap
as they caught the beat.

They danced,
their bodies and souls
lost in the moment,
now—for the moment—in the here—
neither regrets nor worries.

Dance does that,
pulls us beyond time's past and future,
drawing us into the eternal now.

They danced,
we clapped,
God smiled.

Farewell

As he lay dying he whispered
to his wife of forty-six years:
"You are the center of my universe."
Again his words took her breath away.
And she to him:
"Do you know how much I love you?"
And he to her:
"With every fiber of my being."
Then he died.

When we lie dying
may such an exchange take place—
love speaking to love.

A Short Sermon

Supposedly St. John the Evangelist constantly
gave a six-word sermon.
> —Robert Ellsberg, *All Saints*, 565

They say you said,
on every occasion,
regardless of circumstances:
"Brothers and sisters,
love one another."
A short sermon it was
and eventually tiresome.

They asked, your people,
for another topic, a different theme,
to fit differing occasions,
new circumstances.
Supposedly you replied:
"When you've mastered my first lesson,
then we can move on to a second."

Life Reference

He, the preacher,
spoke of love,
yet said nothing of Mother Teresa
walking the streets of Calcutta.

He spoke of sin,
but made no reference
to King David sleeping with the wife of Uriah.

He spoke of compassion—
of participating in others' joys and sorrows;
again, no connection
with the father (Our Father) of the prodigal son.

Preach to me no more
unless life, real life,
is on your tongue,
in your words.

Under God

"I pledge allegiance . . .
    under God . . ."

Are we
or are we not
under God?

Do we
or do we not
state the fact?

Will we
or will we not
pledge full allegiance?

Exclude God
from our nation
"indivisible,
with liberty and justice for all"
and we have thereby
severed the branch from the vine.

Revelation 3:20

"Listen! I am standing at the door,
knocking; if you hear my voice and
open the door, I will come in to you
and eat with you, and you with me."

Lord, my attention span is brief,
I suffer from spiritual ADD.
Open, please open, the door of my mind,
my heart, lest I remain forever imprisoned.
You come so often,
you knock gently,
be it in the soft summer breeze,
the whisper ("Is anyone home?"),
the shuffle of feet on the worn welcome mat.
I long to sit at table with you,
to break bread,
to hear of what's in your heart.
But the noise within,
the full calendar of often meaningless tasks,
the wax in the ears,
all militate against the door opening,
against the presence of your peace,
the gaze of your love.
Break down the door,
wait no longer upon my response,
be my guest even though uninvited.

Be Fruitful

The Gospel imperative "Be fruitful"
—when lived gives glory to God—
is being fulfilled in spades
these August days.
Superabundant the cucumbers,
extravagant the pole beans,
lush the tomatoes.
The whole garden is fecund.
Even the raccoons cannot devour all the sweet corn
and the self-important-looking groundhog
has had its fill of beet tops and lettuce.
All of nature is oozing with life,
teeming, overspilling with glory.
If "ripeness is all,"
then all is here.

Would that my soul
were in its August season.
Then to God would be double glory,
from nature and from me.

Smiled At

Three-years-old he is,
a sidekick to his mother.
Whenever he sees me, he smiles.
His face lights up
like a morning glory
or a sunflower in mid-August.
He knows not my flaws
and if he did, he could care less.
He smiles; I'm smiled at—
I think I'm beginning to learn about grace.

Undoing

Jesus' gaze undid Peter
and the tears flowed.

Jesus' glance undid Zaccheus
and a table was set.

Jesus' look of love undid Mary
and her heart was baptized.

It's all about being seen, being loved,
this Christian journey.
It's all about "undoing,"
being set free by Love.

Todo-Nada

Here is the coin carried by John of the Cross.
On one side: todo—everything—the gift.
On the other: nada—nothing—vacant space.
He fingered this penny every day,
touched the gift of God's impinging love,
caressing the pain and suffering of empty space.
Well worn, this copper piece,
calluses on both thumb and forefinger.

John was in touch with the mystery,
the paradox of everything and nothing,
of life coming through Jesus
and a dying unto oneself.

Markings

On rereading Dag Hammarskjöld's *Markings*

So many negotiations recorded here
between you and your soul,
between you and God.
So much loneliness
for one in the public square.
So much questioning,
hunting for meaning,
for one degreed in law and economics.
So much struggle
in one who was an agent of peace.

And your deepest desire?
Was it the one noted on page ninety-three:
"If only I may grow: firmer, simpler—quieter, warmer."
Your wish has become my prayer.
May my "Yes" be as sound as yours.

Life

For me, life is a garden,
several miles east of Eden.
It has been given in trust—
the owner, an eternity away
yet, somehow, always near.
Every season, every day
I'm tested in every way
to care for the harvest.
My garden is plotted:
worship in one corner,
leisure in another.
Then there are relationships,
besides a thousand and one daily duties.

What have I done with my garden?
How do things grow?
Answers to these questions
a matter of destiny, not show.

The End of September

Thirty days has September . . .
yes, April, June, and November.
Thirty days of living—
glorious weather here in the north,
tomato-picking time,
footballs filling the airways,
book clubs re-assembling,
leaves, tired and falling.

Thirty days—another set of weeks
leading to a full month
with a full moon.
All gift—
I pause to reflect and say thank You.

Things That Really Matter

What are they?
Who are they,
        these things that really matter?
Is it winning or losing
        the tennis match,
the mayoral election,
        the state lottery?
Is it success or failure
        in obtaining this or that contract,
        in passing the orals,
        in breaking the high-jump record?

Or is what really matters
        simply loving and being loved
        by one's God,
        by one's companions,
        by one's self?

Mary

Only three things did she do,
this young maiden of Nazareth.

She listened attentively
      —obedient she was to God's word.
She responded wholeheartedly
      —"yes," she said, though afraid and unknowing.
She participated fully
      —total immersion she gave to her son's life.

For this we say,
    "Ave, Maria"
hail to thee our mother and model.
For this we say,
    "Sancta Maria"
holy are you, our loving, beloved one.

Depth

We walked and talked.
It was a five-mile hike up the knobs of Kentucky.
The inclines were steep,
our conversation roaming:
nature, books, poets, history, personalities.
Nothing sustained, nothing in depth.

Such is my life.
Skimming the surface of this and that,
never settling down to extract all the nectar
from this flower, from this text.
In the end, the honey is thin.
In the end, the wine drunk much too soon.

The Color of Gratitude

My choice is purple,
    recalling the clover in a boyhood meadow.
                                Deo gratias!
Others might chose red,
    watching the fireball sun sink into the ocean.
                                Deo gratias!
Still others opt for blue,
    robin-egg blue telling of hidden life.
                                Deo gratias!

Gratitude is a rainbow,
    sun and rain sharing the same room.
Gratitude is a peanut-butter sandwich (toasted),
    knowing that it is enough.
Gratitude is to dwell in mystery,
    the enigma of being loved,
      of just being.

Save

I sit staring at my computer screen.
A roll of icons offer options—
     print, spell check, save.
I guide the arrow to the last and click.
Whatever I've entered flies to a disc for lodging.

I sit before life,
making decisions hour after hour.
I'm learning, late in life,
to "save" each one,
clicking it to the Center,
referring all to God.

Yet, a difference exists
between "save" and being saved.
By sending all to the divine lodging
it is there transformed and made holy.

In Praise of Enoughness

Such cravings criss-cross my soul.
Insatiable hungers for books,
friendships, spiritual spheres,
excellence in sports, yet another MS,
this poem.
Will it never end,
this thirst for more?

Enough already.
Basta!
Accept the sunbeam
and seek no more.
Tennyson's flower in the crannied wall
deserves a lifetime of reflection.
This hour, like Blake's grain of sand,
contains eternity.

Oh, for the grace of peace,
the gift of silence,
the joy of the here and now,
the ecstasy of thisness.

Presence

It has to do with "here" and "now,"
　　this thing called "presence."
Like the silence sitting at the end of my pen,
or the sweater keeping me winter warm,
or the naked trees outside my February window.
The silence,
　　　the sweater,
　　　　　the trees,
are all here, now.

But I long for a deeper presence,
one that is transcendent,
one that is near.
Some call it the presence of grace.
I call it absence of fear.

Hurry

On thin ice, speed is of the essence.
But in the living of life,
swiftness diminishes presence,
short-changing experience of its due.
Survival may be achieved
but full life may pass us by.
Slow down, my soul,
refuse the haste that kills.
Drink deeply the morning dew;
touch tenderly the evening stars.

A Vision of Prayer

On reading Brigid E. Herman's *Creative Prayer*

Prayer is about discourse,
conversation between friends
that is loving and trusting.

Prayer is about communion,
a humble, simple oneness,
overflowing with creative energy.

Prayer frees us from self-regard,
from slavery to the opinion that others have about us,
from the lies of pride.

Prayer is presence
to the Fountain of being
and the Sustainer of all life.

Out of the Depth

I'm stuck,
stuck in the valley of doubt,
the desert of suspicion.
The magic is all gone.
No longer are ships romantic
nor farms free of manure.
Teachers, once so omniscient,
lack true wisdom and, in fact,
are guilty often of being misinformed.
Gurus, too, be they religious or political,
speak out of an intrinsic poverty.
What a dilemma:
to give up magic
for the forbidden fruit of suspicion.
But one need not stay in darkness.
Wonder and awe can come with dawn
if we have a modicum of hope,
a tinge of simple faith.

My Accuser

He said to me:
"You live high off the hog!"
How can this be,
me being a vegetarian?
Pork is not on my menu,
just lettuce,
potatoes and tomatoes,
and lovely pole beans.

"High off the hog!"
My accuser is merciless.
Just now another accusation fell—
that I lack imagination.

All this I would disregard quickly
were it not that my accuser is God.

Addiction

What is it?
A moral lapse?
A disease?
Or, something else?

The "it" is addiction—
be it to alcohol,
tobacco, cybersex,
or Orville Redenbacher's gourmet popping corn,
or chocolate.

The experts say it's a disease
while others name it sin.
Whatever,
freedom is diminished, if not absent;
and the addict is trapped, severely impaired.

Last night an addict spoke,
telling his story of enslavement to booze
and, by so doing, set us free.

Discreet Festivity

"But this festivity must also remain discreet,
lest it insult the immense pain of millions of
women and men who throughout the world
continue to live in despair."
  —Louis-Marie Chauvet, *The Sacraments*, 101

No wet-blanket here,
just high sensitivity for those who suffer
while we enjoy—
        enjoy the wine at Cana,
        enjoy the sudden gift of friendship.
        enjoy the surgery restoring health.

Be discreet in these festivities.
Yes, dance and sing and be merry
but, before falling asleep,
remember unto the Lord all those,
millions upon millions,
who have no wine or friends,
who live near the edge of despair.

Wad

"Shoot your wad!" they say.
Is this mere barbershop wisdom,
bumper-sticker philosophy,
or is it solid advice?

Good writers never save.
They spend what is given daily,
confident that the morrow
will bring its own wealth.

Lecturers speak what comes to mind.
No holding back a story or quote
for a more auspicious time
that probably will never come.

So, "shoot your wad!"
Write and speak and live what you know.
Trust that tomorrow the spring will still flow
with even purer, colder, fresher water.

A Cathedral Brick

"Add your brick to the cathedral of life,"
they say.
But brick upon brick makes no home,
event upon event piled high, no life.
A design is needed,
a game plan—a life plan.

Our vocation is architecture,
a double calling to envision and execute.
Our vocation is to align our mission,
to place our brick
into the hand of the Master builder.
It is in this submission
that Chartres became a reality.

Efficacy

Are words efficacious?
Do words work?
Do they transform
and are they fruitful?

Words like "I love you,"
or "You're forgiven,"
or "Please forgive me"?

Words like "help,"
or "wow," or "oops"?

And God's word,
    God's Word,
efficacious or not?

Ponder the Cross.

Lodge! Feed! Move!

"Considerable attention was paid to knowledge of the Bible
in the childhood of most of us here, no doubt in the hope that
what was lodged in the mind would feed the heart and move
the will."—Robert Llewelyn, *Thirsting for God,* 92

What words are lodged in my mind?
What is it that feeds my longing heart?
What moves my will toward noble deeds?

Two words!

The first, "horizons,"
mentally shoves me toward Eternity.
Affectively, it nourishes and expands my heart.
Behaviorally, it opens me to acres of spaciousness.

A second word, "gratitude."
All is gift, my mind informs me.
My heart senses a loving presence behind each offer.
And generosity becomes the only possible response.

My soul, keep a holy lexicon near at hand.
Find a daily word,
one to lodge, feed, and move me
lest I wither away.

The Cup

It must be held,
firmly, gently, yes, gratefully.
It's the cup of joys and sorrows,
life in its entirety.
Then, once held, lifted,
toasting our compassionate God
who sweated and wept in a garden,
but danced at a wedding in Cana.
Finally, the test comes in the drinking,
down to the dregs,
whatever the liquid given,
scalding or iced.

Can we drink of the cup?
Did James and John really do it?

Mary did,
and now lives in glory.

The Center

We thought the sun the center of the universe.
      Wrong!
We thought the hub the center of the wheel.
      Wrong!
We thought the ego the center of existence.
      Wrong!

All is circumference
except for the One.

All is peripheral
except for the Essential.

All is as naught
except for the All.

The February Sun

Sitting in my rocker facing east,
I suddenly saw the February sun burst through the blinds,
race across the room
filling my face with light.
I squinted, the sunshine too much,
and as I did so,
a hundred rays danced in all directions.
I rode one back across the room,
out the window,
and across millions of miles of space.
I almost reached the sun
but it had moved slightly to the south.
So, I headed home,
as quickly as I had gone,
exhausted but exhilarated by this moment of grace.

Walden

Too much detail.
Too much talk of rods and ice-making,
loons and rabbits,
beans, and more beans, and yet still more.

Yet I'm back again to your small parlor
needing to hear
the call to simplicity,
the power of nature's healing,
the grace of silence,
the gift of solitude.

I'm back again to ponder
the desperate lives of men,
the invasion of technology,
the pretty toys of our inventions.

Would I were as awake as you,
a noticer of everything great and small.

Envy

It's not their beauty I envy,
those frogs down at the creek.
Rather, it's the ability
to straddle two worlds.
Comfortable they are on land or sea,
something foreign to bird or bee.

And my two worlds?
Time and Eternity!
When in one, I long for the other;
when in the other, my heart is elsewhere.

Is there some philosophic frog
who, with quiet patience,
might teach me his art
and drain the envy from my heart?

Sprague/Cambodia

Do

Do!
Do something!
Do something
    "beautiful for God."
Thus spoke Mother Teresa of Calcutta.
The something?
        a cup of cold water
        a robe of compassion
        a pat on the back
        a smile across a subway aisle
        a birthday phone call
        a vote for life
        the planting of a tree

Do something "beautiful for God!"
Do something!
Do!

Be!

Easter——2005

Easter lilies—what beauty!
Easter eggs—hidden and found, what fun!
Easter bonnets—how cute!
Easter bunnies—catch them if you can!

Yet more is needed here,
here in the place so close to the Cross,
so near to an empty tomb,
right next to broken lives.

We need Easter eyes
to see life in the midst of death,
forgiveness for sins of betrayal and torture,
glory in the blood of the Passion.

Lilies and eggs, bonnets and bunnies
offer a surface joy.
It's Easter "Alleluias"
—our praise of the Risen Lord—
that flood our hearts with lasting joy.

A River

A river runs through it,
through my soul,
deep, deep within.
Beside the river is a log,
whereon the Lord sits,
always,
waiting.
I cannot see his face,
I cannot feel his touch,
but he is there,
waiting,
always.

Today I journeyed within,
sat on the log,
by the river,
waiting.
All there was was silence,
yes, Silence.

Seeing the Painting

Crawl, if you can,
into the tiny corner of the picture,
the one on the opposite wall,
the one Rembrandt painted of the prodigal son.
Can you feel the son's shame,
the father's extravagant compassion,
the ire of the elder son?
Be still: take it all in.

Crawl out
and take with you the grace of homecoming,
the joy of reconciliation,
the music of the feast in the background and
the peace that filled a broken home.

Crawling into the corner of a picture
to watch, to listen—
let's call it contemplation.

Tiptoe

I'm flat-footed.
Thus my vision is limited,
my horizon just inches in front of my nose.

I've been advised to stand on tiptoe,
to raise my sights to things eternal,
those far-off things in the land of infinity.

I tried.
I tried every morning
but my toes failed me.

All I see,
in my flat-footed world,
are daisies, finches, and bumble bees.

I told my advisor
that that was enough for me.

Hope

". . . the art of wise forgetting."—Evelyn Underhill

Is there wisdom in forgetting,
forgetting the trivial,
 the superfluous,
  the inane?
Like the missed free throw in the championship game,
or the blunder in the graduation talk,
or the planting of the tulips upside down?
These memories foster self-absorption,
blind us to the present,
waste tons of energy.

To be an artist of wise forgetting
is to become an agent of hope.

Mountaineers

Are you called to the mountains?
To Mount Everest
or the small hill behind the house?
Some are called to the prairie;
others, to the shore of the sea.

Whatever,
listen to the call
and set out immediately.

Moses came to the edge of the promised land
yet did not gain entry.

So be it!
In the end it's not about a place—
a mountain, a sea, or even a prairie.
It's about being in union with the Caller,
who is the only Geography of lasting peace.

Beyond Me

Almost everything is beyond me:
the inner workings of a combustion engine,
the DNA helix,
the orbiting of planets,
how gravity and grace work,
the flight of a bumblebee.

Is there anything that I truly comprehend?
Anything that is not beyond me?

One thing alone,
one thing I understand:
the kindness behind being given
a cup of water,
a word of affirmation,
a smile across a subway aisle.

They Is

Who can comprehend the mystery of the Trinity?
The greatest minds have tried,
and stumbled,
and ultimately failed.

A third-grader,
after hearing about God (one in three persons)
as Creator, Redeemer, Sanctifier,
as Giver, Given, Giving,
as Life, Light, Love,
simply said,
"Oh, you mean, They is."

They is,
a triune Being.
Need more be said?

Exile

What is your native land,
that place where you are truly at home?
I speak here not of geography,
that space where latitude and longitude intersect.
Rather, the question is one of gift,
the question of when (not where)
you are most alive, fully engaged,
all else drudgery except this moment in time
breaking through into eternity.

Yesterday I came home,
wrote for three hours,
experienced a modicum of peace.

Now a new day has come
and I'm off to the races,
back into the land of exile.

Artist-Lover

Prayer is "to stand beside the Artist-Lover
and to see what he sees."—Evelyn Underhill

All day I sat beside the Artist-Lover,
the God revealed in Jesus,
and scanned the horizon.
My seeing changed,
my hearing and feelings too.
Clouds were his sighs
and stars his promise of light.
The pasta at table,
the full, low moon,
and the afternoon wind storm—
all epiphanies of divine power.
While I sat quietly the milieu became divine,
everything regained its "dearest freshness."

Now I'm back on the road,
my seeing blurred,
my hearing impaired.
I must, come day's end,
hurry back to my Artist-Lover
to regain my sight and hope.

Conversion

On the road,
having fallen to the ground,
Saul turned into Paul.

Under a tree,
finding God's word,
Augustine was set free.

Though seeming sudden,
turning from idols
and clarifying desires
—the process of conversion—
take time, God's time
that we call eternity.

Monasticism

What is it like
to live in a cloister?
I've been asked to write
of this way of life, an outsider.
How can a foreigner
convey an atmosphere of silence,
its joys and terrors?
How can an alien
speak of the rule and routine,
living on a permissive planet?
How can an accidental tourist
speak of community and poverty and obedience,
driving down life's fast lane?

Yet are we not all alike,
the monk and post-modern man?
Struggling pilgrims all,
pursued by that loving hound of heaven,
that prodigal father running down
life's dusty road to embrace us.

Theology-on-Tap

There were just five of us
sitting at a sports bar
talking of theology, things divine.
A travel agent, an analyst,
a software engineer, a teacher,
and me, a man of the cloth.
Things divine?
Divorce and adoption,
spiritual direction and books,
friendship and prayer,
tsunami and hurricanes.

We had gone to a church
but the doors were locked.
The bar was open
and with a beer or two, minds too.
We sat for hours talking theology,
of things divine, of life lived.

Odell/USA

Joy

It's like the wind
    blowing now here, now there,
    wherever people care,
    wherever the right thing is done
        in the right way.

It's like sunshine,
    falling on every flower, every atom,
    so that petals open and expand
    and every atom dances,
        doing handstands.

It's like an infant's smile,
    tickled into laughter,
    hugged into life,
    wrapped in the warmth
        of a grandma's arms.

Joy is like
    a love-letter
    carried next to the heart.

Enough

Satisfaction!
Satis: the Latin for enough.
Why are we never satisfied?
Why this insatiability?
Indeed, this perpetual dissatisfaction?

I've been trying, for over sixty years,
to retrieve the word enough.
Enough stuff! Enough pleasure! Enough prestige!
Yet the warfare goes on and on and on
with the major combatants being
"More" versus "Enough."

Under which banner, my soul,
will you stand?

Mindfulness

When one looks deeply—
    into the heart of a budding hibiscus,
    at a full moon rising,
    under the words of affection—
        mindfulness!

When nothing is slighted or taken for granted—
    snowflakes falling on one's tongue,
    a smile across a subway aisle,
    the breeze gently touching summer leaves—
        mindfulness!

When hurry is denied and time is taken,
when breathing is deep and food is truly tasted,
when all is done with gentle deliberation—
        mindfulness!

Living Buddha, Living Christ

On reading Thich Nhat Hanh's *Living Buddha, Living Christ*

It's all about "deeply"
—this thing called mindfulness —
to see deeply,
to understand deeply,
to love deeply.

It's about the capacity to be here,
present to the moment,
breathing in and out with gentle awareness.

It's about experiencing the now,
each successive moment with a quiet yes.

It's about living—
living Buddha, living Christ.

On the Death Anniversary
of Jessica Powers

Eighteen years ago the poet died
and yet she lives.
Just yesterday someone wrote in gratitude
for the poet's "The Homecoming."
Just yesterday I recited from memory
her verse "The Garments of God."
So, though dead, she lives
and speaks to us of death and mercy,
cedar trees and sparrows,
Abraham and Mary.

But it's more than words,
more than a distinctive voice from the past.
She herself lives
having been welcomed home
and embraced by a God of grace.

It's an anniversary not of a death
but of a life full grown.

Full of Grace

Archbishop Carlo Maria Martini wrote that
"full of grace" means "You have been loved
for a very long time."

How long have you been loved?
Give me your age and add nine months.
That's how long.
At this very moment—now—
you are being loved,
loved into existence,
loved unto death.

We've all heard the common expression:
"He/she just doesn't get it."

I'm one of those.
When will I get it—
get the insight that I
have been loved for a very long time?
Get the fact that all of us
are full of grace,
beloved and cared for?

Maybe tomorrow?

Woo

Is wooing a lost art?
Booing certainly isn't.
In a culture of complaint,
hissing is everywhere.

So who is the woo-er;
who, the woo-ed?

Jesus is the paradigm
pursuing Zacchaeus in Jericho,
the wedding couple in Cana,
Saul on the road to Damascus.

Was Emily Dickinson right
in her belief that
if there is no wooing in heaven
what a dull place it would be?

It cannot be dull
for God is the one who woos
and we are the subject of divine affection.

Creative Prayer

On rereading Brigid E. Herman's *Creative Prayer*

It's so many things,
this life of creative prayer.
A pilgrimage, surely, from self to God;
communion with the Lord in words and silence;
a movement from the circumference to the center;
high commerce between the human and the divine;
God's creative energy transforming humanity;
a divine science of waiting in solitude;
a mutual hospitality;
the habit of referring everything to God;
a great adventure into the mysteries of faith;
a liberal education that grants no degrees.

It's really just one thing,
this life of creative prayer:
Love encountering love.

Our On-Going Incarnation

On reading Michael Himes's *On-Going Incarnation*

A heavy tome here,
packed full of dense theology,
weighted with abstract terms,
yet in a prose accessible to most.

And the lessons learned in the reading?
Creation is the first revelation.
Experience demands reflection
   and translates feelings into concepts.
Apprehension of God is contingent
   upon one's spiritual horizon.
The kingdom of God is Christianity's master idea.
"Holiness is one with love."
The mutual penetration of opposing forces
   is the secret of all true life.
"The fact that anything exists is
   a statement of divine love."

And the bottom line:
the Incarnation is on-going—
divinity taking on flesh
all over the place.

We need eyes to see—
ears to hear—
the invasions of grace.

Gettysburg Address

November 19, 1863

It was but a three-minute discourse
after the main orator's two-hour dissertation.
Yet your words, old Abe, live on:
"Four score and seven years ago . . ."

Just four months before,
fifty thousand (dead or wounded)
littered the orchard and hillsides
on Seminary Ridge and Cemetery Hill.

Your words consecrated the grounds.
No, the blood of the fallen did that
and you simply spoke of what was.

More than "four score and seven years ago"
we remember what you said
    and cry.

Late Night Walk

I was alone again.
Well, not really.
The Big Dipper was there
and the darkness.
They did not speak.
I was held by silence.

It was a long walk into the country.
Only three cars were about
and they quickly came and went.
The darkness and the stars remained.

Returning home, I found
people conversing,
the television blaring,
books reaching out to be read.

Outside,
the stars and darkness abided,
faithful to the grace of silence.

Daddy

I stood with their dad at the end of the hall
talking of maintenance things.
His two daughters,
both pre-kindergarteners,
came around the corner and spotted him.
    "Daddy,
    Daddy,"
they cried out and ran toward him.

It wasn't as if
they had been separated for months, even days.
Earlier that morning they had breakfasted together.

But for a two- and a four-year-old,
even an hour of being apart
can feel like eternity.

I stood next to their dad
as they passed me in their race
to hug their father,
all the way up to his knees.

Never will I forget hearing
that double melody of "Daddy, Daddy,"
nor will I forget
the delight in their father's eyes.

O Rex Gentium

O Antiphon—December 22

We, in democratic countries,
have banished all kings.
We, in a secular culture,
dismiss divine longings,
a deity holding all things together.
Our salvation lies in power
and prestige and possessions.
Though haunted by mortality,
we construct gold idols out of clay.

What then if God comes
into our dark, exhausted world?
Will we be saved despite our ignorance,
our foolish, unfounded arrogance?

O Holy Night, come!

Gethsemane

Jesus, this was your garden,
Gethsemane.
Here you tasted anguish,
torment of the soul,
the poverty of our human condition.
You asked to be spared;
you prayed that the Father's will be done.

And your disciples slept.

But you do not sleep
when we go into our gardens of sorrow.
You are there
to give us courage,
to guide us on our way.

We sweat blood together.

Only One

"You need only one person
who loves you . . .
that's all you need."

This comment made, in passing,
over bacon and eggs:
to be loved,
to be the center of another's attention,
to be affirmed,
made to feel
important.

And only one person needed.

After the toast and coffee,
I whispered under my breath: "Amen!"

Sprague/Brazil

Gossip

"gossip n. gossyp; also godsip; late As. godsibbe, baptismal sponsor, godparent; see God & Sib"——Mr. Webster

The town gossip is no godparent,
surely not one's baptismal sponsor.
Rather, he/she indulges in idle talk,
in rumors about others,
often with an edge of superiority,
if not disdain.

I sat for years on a personnel board.
For three hours, once a month,
we chatted and chatted and chatted about others.
Idle talk?
Rumors?
Responsible dialogue?
Smart-ass remarks?
Perceptive analysis?
Sound evaluation?
Snide, cutting jibes?

I hope Peter
(the one at the gate)
works alone, sans personnel board.
I hope that Peter and God
have dispensed with peer evaluation.

Kyrie eleison!

Roots

On watching "The Roots of Vatican II," a video by Michael Himes

He sat at his lonely desk,
refuting now thoughts some forty years old.
It was an act of humility
done in service to the truth.
His name, John Henry Newman;
his refutation, *Via Media.*

But all that is retrospective.
More important, his prospective thoughts.
He wrote about the mission of the Church,
the mission of Jesus:
priestly, prophetic, kingly.

Almost a century later
these thoughts bore fruit,
shaping an ecumenical council,
molding a new sense of identity
for a Christian people.

Here lies the roots of Vatican II,
for here was born a glorious vision.

Broken Record

The needle rested in the rut
as the record turned round and round and round.

Whoever said there is no purgatory?
The same refrain repeated
again and again and again.

And my life?
A broken record?
The same routine
season after season after season?

And yet,
the music is not redundant.
The record is not broken,
so I need but nudge
the needle to the next groove . . .

Mental Toughness

Thoughts ought not be given free rein.
Like emotions, even deeds,
they can scramble for sovereignty.
Something seeking to run the show,
to be in charge, to play king of the mountain.
The struggle can be incessant.

Softness is permissive:
any idea, feeling, action can rule the roost.
Toughness is discipline:
holding in check whatever diminishes life.

Mental, emotional, behavioral toughness!
Yes!
Not hardness of heart,
but a grace making peace possible.

"A Patch of Holiness, Please"

Our torn, tattered history needs patching,
pieces of love to cover the tears,
fabric of affection to heal our hardness of heart.
And patches have come.
Francis mended his times with troubadour songs,
Mother Teresa, with her hospice care.
Patches of love holding together
whole nations on the edge of disintegration.

Whether Italy or India,
Wall Street or the monastery,
the halls of parliament or the university dorm,
Baghdad or Darfur,
we need a patch of holiness,
a light to shine in our dark universe.

Delight

Does God delight in us,
flawed, finite, faltering creatures?

Yesterday a theologian
(one who "studies" God)
took us into academic spheres,
our minds reeling with theological abstractions.
But then he told a story,
the making of pizza with his four young sons.
Two pounded flour high into the air
while the other two,
with kettles on their heads,
charged one another like medieval knights.
Our theologian, the father,
had but one word for the
noisy, chaotic, rambunctious experience:
        "Delight!"
We left the conference hall laden
with theological insights
about a God who is everywhere,
in the making of pizzas,
in ancient-young warriors in kitchen battles,
in people gathered to reflect on God's grace.
I left with but one word:
        "Delight"
a delight God has for us
as a father for his sons.

Juan Diego

And Mary came—
and all was different.

She was your Gabriel
announcing compassion to your people.
She, the Mother of the Lord,
proclaimed God's love
and a Church arose.

Mary went—
and you went forth on mission,
an "old pile of sticks"
doing God's work.

And a people was born.

JUAN DIEGO of MEXICO

Threshold

An invisible line surrounds us.
Though unseen it's as real
as one that is drawn in the sand.
Cross it,
and we are in a new realm
be it war with another nation,
entanglement in a love affair,
blessedness of God's life and grace.

Mary crossed the threshold with her "fiat,"
Abelard and Heloise in their embrace,
the founding fathers in the Declaration of Independence.

Each of us decides—perhaps each day—
to cross or remain behind that invisible line,
that threshold into a new horizon
that forever changes our destiny.

Making

We are makers, bakers,
busy constructing as creators.
We make music,
babies,
hay (while the sun shines),
and, oh yes, moonshine.

It was Jesus who said,
"Go, make disciples!"
Ah, this is the tough one:
the making of caring,
loving, forgiving creatures.

Of course, it begins at home,
this making of servants;
it begins at the kitchen table
and in the doing of dishes.

First Communion

First anything!
   Do you remember
   your first kiss,
   your first date,
   your first bike,
   your first airplane ride,
   your first sin,
   your first communion?

The door swings open
and your world is changed,
for good, for ill.

And then there are the "lasts"—
   the last day of school,
   the last day at work,
   the last goodbye hug,
   the last breath and heartbeat,
   the last . . .

Beginnings and endings—
and then there's Eternity.

So What?

Don't be dismissive, my soul.
Don't underestimate the smallest word,
the simplest event of the day.
Anoint every encounter;
appreciate every gesture;
honor every glance.

It's in the ordinary,
the mundane, the routine,
that grace resides.
See it! Cherish it!

And then give thanks.

There is no other path to peace;
no other road to joy.

The Color of Sin

Why is sin scarlet
(as in "The Scarlet Letter")
or why crimson?
And why is grace white,
as white as snow, as white as wool?

If the Deity had asked me
I would have chosen green,
as in envy.
Perhaps, even black
as in moods and meanness.
Even orange would do,
on days of cowardice.

But God's crayons are few,
    just two—
        red and white.

No arguing with the Divine Artist.

Lost Christianity

On reading Jacob Needleman's
Lost Christianity: A Journey of Rediscovery

The search is on,
always has been,
for that "someone," that "something"
that is missing.
It's not that it's not here.
Rather, something obstructs
our experiences—
the being here, the Now.
What's needed?
What's missing?
What's lost?
The art of attentiveness—
the being open, sensitive, present.

"Hide-and-go-seek"
is the human game
played every hour of every day.

Moon

Can one fall in love with the moon?
It's a cold, chunky blot of matter in space.
And yet, on these warm September nights,
the orb holds me in fascination.
Each evening it unveils more and more of itself
in circular revelations striving toward fullness.
Victory last night came in perfect circularity.
Its orangeness meshed well with a lovely pumpkin patch.
Its silence competed brilliantly with the stars.
Its beauty made artists weep.

I have fallen in love with the moon.
Her wooing won my soul.

True Resurrection

On reading H. A. Williams's *True Resurrection*

Resurrection happens daily,
wherever life emerges
from the artist's dry paint,
or a friendship is reborn,
or the daffodil's shyness ends.

Fix your gaze not on future life
but on the now of creation,
a now that even death cannot stop.
Listen to the silent music
singing of unity, not division,
hope, not despair.

If you need to talk about
the "how" of resurrection,
stand beneath an oak tree
when acorns fall to their new earth home
or watch the flight of a butterfly.

Call 337- . . . .

It's a long, lonely drive
from Wisconsin to New Jersey.
Lonely and long, too, the discernment process,
to be, to do, this or that.
Now thirty years of age
he felt called to ministry,
committed to serve the Lord and God's people.

Midway through Ohio,
he stopped for the night at the local motel.
Mourning the loss of friends back home,
weary of travel,
anxious about the future,
he picked up the ubiquitous Gideon Bible.
It listed scriptural passages for various circumstances:
   "If you are happy, read . . ."
   "If troubled, read . . ."
   "If lonely, turn to . . ."

Ah, his loneliness addressed by God's word.
He turned to the prophet Jeremiah quickly
and read the poignant passage
regarding God's consolation.

Almost to the end of the designated passage
he turned the page to read an insert:
"If you are still lonely,
phone 337 - . . . ."

A Preacher

Fr. Frank McNulty gave a parish
mission here at Resurrection Parish,
Green Bay—April 3-5, 2006

He was one year shy of eighty.
His steps were short,
his body gradually growing frail.
But not his voice,
not his preaching the Gospel
through stories and humor and conviction.
He was low-key,
no shouting people out of hell,
no condemning the stray,
no attacking the morally wounded.
He preached yet another parish mission,
going for the heart
while enriching the mind and imagination.
He preached Jesus,
the one who manifested a loving God,
the one who took on our suffering.
He was one year shy of eighty,
and still making us laugh and cry
on our journey back to God.

Awry

Such is life—awry.
As in "not straight"—
    the cabinet door that doesn't close,
    the left eye slightly off center,
    thinking "askew" means "ajar."

Such is life—awry.
As in "amiss"—
    plans gone haywire,
    the trumpet too sharp, too flat,
    a love, like milk, turned sour.

Such is life—awry.
As in "wrong"—
    more money means happiness,
    victory equals peace,
    one's name on the marquee is glory,

Pungent

Pungent was the night,
a May night rich with lilacs abloom.
It took my breath away
like when a lover enters the room.
If you've never been smitten by spring,
there's little you'll understand,
if anything.

Fault Finding

The left eye was operative,
the one that finds faults,
that is critical and negative,
that is moody, yes, nasty.

This time it spotted
high formality,
pious pretense,
a loud, unpleasant voice,
non-recognition.

And the right eye,
the one that sees beauty,
runs to gratitude,
rejoices in effort?
It was dormant, inoperative,
half-asleep.

So, the heart was joyless
since the dominant left eye
controlled the vision,
one's fate that day.

Surprised by Joy

On rereading C. S. Lewis's *Surprised by Joy:*
The Shape of My Early Life

What is it that shapes years?
For C. S. Lewis, a major element was joy,
that Desire, that stab, that longing
that arose from music and mythology,
hills and solitary paths, nature and goodness.
Joy was a by-product, a signpost
pointing toward something, Someone eternal.
Lewis's whole story was a history of joy—
its presence in good teachers, books, and friends;
its absence in the lack of love and truth.
Life is shaped by so many factors,
none greater than the Northernness of grace,
the subtle intrusions of God,
that transcendental Interferer,
that divine Love
for whom our hearts long and yearn.

Sunday Evening Walk

It was a Sunday evening walk,
a walk down to the river,
the Fox River where I dipped
my hand into the brown goddess.
I looked to the north
where the river ran to the bay
and then on to Lake Michigan
heading toward the mighty ocean.
I looked to the south
from whence the river came,
from the deeper interior of Wisconsin
and beyond.

I touched the river,
once pure, now polluted
but striving to give life.

It did just that to my soul
on a Sunday evening walk down to the river.

Trinity

Try wrapping your arms around a great redwood tree
or, in a glance, take in the whole mountain range,
or, on the ocean shore, touch the horizon.
Good luck.
Failure here is inevitable.

The preacher takes a stab at the Trinity,
attempting some degree of illumination.
His arms are too short,
his glance too swift,
his ambition too bold.

We leave the church nearly
 as ignorant as we came.
And yet,
knowledge yields to love
and we might thereby be one inch
closer to our infinite loving Triune God.

The "How" of Presence

How do we remain present,
truly being where we are—here and now?
How do we remain mindful,
truly aware of
    the song of the mourning dove,
    the jam on the toast,
    the hope in the heart for peace?

Too often we are absent,
inattentive, unaware, insensitive.
We awake one day and discover
that life has passed us by.

So "how,"
how to connect with the moment?
Conversation!
Dialogue with the dove, the jam, the hope.
Speak to them, listen to their message.
Language it is that makes most things present
and, in-between the words, the silence.

Cautions

On reading Douglas Steere

As Adam and Eve departed Eden,
journeying to the east,
two cautions were posted at the gate.
The first read: "Overactivity!"
The second: "Underattention!"

Such warnings remain to our day.
Busy beavers are we,
pragmatic to the extreme,
idolizing our life of activism.

And then there is attention deficit,
a disorder universal in nature,
deadly to the quality of life.

I just spotted Adam in a hammock
and Eve quietly gazing out of the kitchen window.
Since leaving Eden,
they're back on the road to recovery.

Let It Be Written

Why write?
Why get out pen and pad,
chain oneself to a desk,
wait on the muses,
dwell in solitude
while the rest of the world simply
frolics to and fro?

Prestige?
Money?
To stem the tide of time?
Why, why write?

The psalmist had a motive:
"Let this be written for ages to come,
that a people yet unborn may praise the Lord."

Ps. 102:18

Privacy

Can one have be too much privacy?
Thomas Merton thought so—
as in "not to be known by God."
For him, that was simply
too much privacy.

How to balance the public and the private?
How to know the limits of appropriate self-revelation?

Such balance,
such knowing/being known
is part of the art of living.

One thing seems certain:
"Not to be known by God is too much privacy."
But that is impossible.
And here is the grace:
God's knowing is always God's loving.

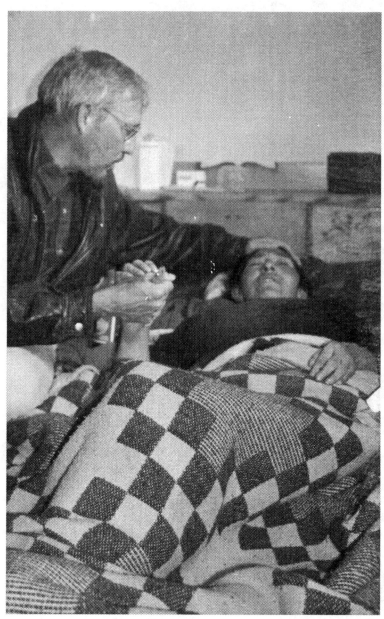

Teachers

Along life's journey, teachers emerge.
Their titles vary: spiritual directors,
coaches, mentors.
Their methods too: direct or indirect,
stern or gentle, demanding or patient.

Another instructor came this week: Pain!
The lesson: "Your passing pain
for many is a chronic condition
Therefore, have compassion."

I pray that I do not forget
how suffering holds us captive.
I pray that I have compassion
for all the suffering ones.

"Open"

The sign hung inside the window:
    "Open"
With a flick of a wrist
and one quick turn, the sign now read:
    "Closed."

We've seen the sign
on business doors,
libraries,
even churches.
Public facilities have their days and seasons
of availability and closure.

As God walks the universe
and encounters human souls,
a sign hangs at the entrance
of every mind, of every heart.

Is it "Open" or "Closed"?

The Lord awaits our decision.

While Walking

While walking in the darkness of late evening,
on a warm, balmy summer night,
I stopped and stood in the wind.
It was gentle,
almost soft.
There was no quiet, whispering sound;
only silence.
Yet it was not devoid of music,
the music of presence,
of blessed assurance
that we are not alone in the universe.

Where the wind came from, I do not know.
That it came and greeted me, I am certain.

I continued my evening walk,
no longer lonely,
but accompanied,
accompanied, now, in all that I do.

Assuming the Assumption

Why, why the long delay?
Why wait nearly two thousand years
to proclaim Mary's assumption into heaven?
Should not the assumption have been assumed
from the moment Mary said, "Yes"
to the noble Gabriel,
or "Do whatever he tells you"
to the dumbfounded waiter,
or (her greatest discourse)
standing silently beneath the cross?

In truth, the assumption was assumed
for nigh two thousand years.
It was only fifty years ago
that what was assumed
was officially spoken.

Adam

Adam, tell me of the God
with whom you walked in the cool of the evening
in that easy, tender friendship.
Tell me of that original beauty,
all that wholeness and harmony and radiance
that brought joyful tears to your eyes,
that filled you with fullness of life.
Tell me, blessed Adam,
of the particularity of divine providence,
of the art of adoration,
of God's gracious kiss.
Tell me, too, of the fall
as holiness seeped out of your soul
and the lost, pure, unearned joy
that no longer came with the dawn.
Tell me, Adam, of how,
far, far east of Eden,
God's grace continued to anoint you priest,
mediator between heaven and earth.
Tell me, tell me, of that blessed *felix culpa.*

Tell me your story
that I might know my own.

Noah

Noah, tell me, of the flood,
the desecration of the world,
and how, in the ark,
you preserved God's life and peace.
Tell me, too, how you rescued the animals,
how you kept the chaotic sea at bay,
how you sent life out as the waters receded.

Pray for us, noble Noah,
that against the nothingness of our times
we might preserve the order of God's creative love
and, when the wind dies down
and God's glory can again be seen,
we might open the ark's window
and in your Spirit re-create the world.

The Edge

To live on the edge
—the edge of sadness, the edge of joy—
is to be near
but not to possess.

Is it what the masters called hope?

Moses saw the promised land
but did not enter.
He lived on the edge of a promise.

Adam settled down east of Eden,
not far from the garden of paradise.
He died there on the edge of peace.

And you, my soul,
you who live on the edge of nothingness,
know that the promise of peace
is perhaps nearer than your next breath.

Without Music

Imagine, if you will,
a bride coming down the aisle
and the church is devoid of music.
Or, a chase is taking place
in a Western film with no sound track.
And, worst of all,
we live our lives
with no background music.

Someone once wrote
that existence without serious music
would be dreary, verging on deadly.

Always, always, keep a song in your heart,
lest your voice become unmusical.

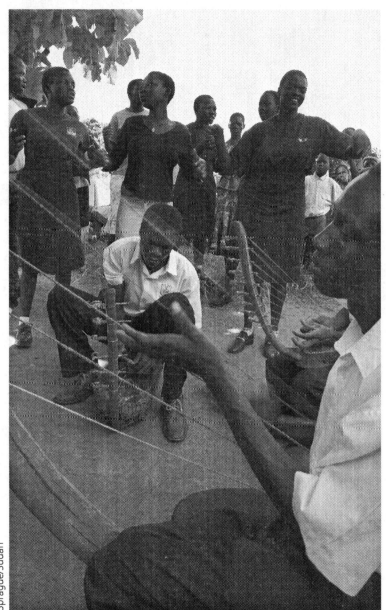

Vacuum

They say,
the erudite scientists,
that nature abhors a vacuum.

They say,
the spiritual masters,
that the soul thrives on emptiness.

I say,
a struggling pilgrim,
that both cannot be right.

Knots

Tying knots can be a vice—
ask any counselor whose refrain is:
"Don't tie yourself up in knots."

If you do that
while sailing through life,
you lose your freedom of spirit.
Then no wind is friendly,
no sunset beautiful,
no blessing a sheer grace.

Tied up in knots
(the knot of self-disdain
or the knot of "never-good-enough"
or the knot of guilt and shame),
we know no peace, no joy.

Unravel the knots
(with help, if necessary)
and let the rope of freedom
swing freely in the wind.

Holy Obedience

Sunflowers are to be envied.
With simple fidelity,
day after summer day,
they follow the sun
as it marches from east to west.
I've yet to see a disobedient one.

But we humans,
gifted with freedom,
need not live in holy obedience.
Rather than follow God's gracious light,
we can rebel,
choosing darkness over light.

I envy sunflowers,
the holy, obedient ones.

Wonders of the World

What is on your list?
What are the wonders of your world?
A friendship of some thirty years?
A view from a mountain top?
A kind word given on a heavy day?

And my wonders?
The lilies of the valley alongside our family garage;
Jessica Powers' poem "The Garments of God";
Beethoven's Sixth Symphony;
the full-moon rising over Chambers Island.

Wonders all . . .
once again I remove my sandals.

Danger

Near our family home,
within a block,
a transforming station took up residence.
On the fence enclosing the power plant
were numerous signs:
"DANGER: HIGH VOLTAGE!"

Just as our bodies face dangers,
so too our souls.
Last night someone said:
"That conversation was dangerous to the soul."

We must beware of spiritual dangers:
images degrading our sexuality;
stories of brutality and violence;
entertainment dissipating our energies.

High voltage all.
If touched, sudden death,
for both body and soul.

Bartimaeus

My name is Bartimaeus.
I'm from Jericho.
I'm poor.
I'm blind.

They tell me
that the sky is blue,
the desert is brown,
the trees are green.

They tell me
that my mother is beautiful,
that stars fill the evening sky,
that mountains are huge.

My poverty is not lack of wealth
but lack of sight.

Then Jesus came,
the seer and the sage.
He took away my poverty;
He took away my blindness.

I left Jericho and followed Him.

The Problem of Fun

"Just as believers in a beneficent deity should be haunted by the problem of natural evil, so agnostics, atheists, pessimists, and nihilists should be haunted by the problem of friendship, love, beauty, truth, humor, compassion, fun. Never forget the problem of fun."

—John Horgan, *Rational Mysticism*, 227

Never, never forget the problem of fun.

How could Jesus at Cana,
make wine and make merry,
with Calvary just around the corner?

How could Anne Frank study her history lesson,
delighting in new knowledge,
with the Nazis just outside her annex window?

How could Lou Gehrig,
knowing the approaching of a painful death,
exclaim: "I'm the luckiest man in the world"?

We've got a problem here,
the problem of joy, delight, "luck."
Never, never forget the problem of fun.

Benediction and Bingo

A thin wall divided the two events:
Eucharistic adoration in the church proper,
bingo in the gathering area.

Silence filled the one space.
Shouts of B-five, I-twenty, and N-forty-two next door.

Yet even with the wall between them
Jesus passed freely from one to the other.

Grace was in the silence, in the reverential awe;
grace was in the playing and in the shout "BINGO!"

As I walked though the gathering area to the church,
the wall seem to have disappeared.

The Edge (2)

The cup and saucer sat on the edge of the counter.
Another inch,
a slight jar,
a door slamming shut
and the cup and saucer would be over the edge,
unto the floor,
shattered in a dozen pieces.

As I walk through life,
the edge is ever present,
for me, for all.
This is where we live,
on the brink of death,
indeed, on the edge of nothingness.

There are here two choices:
constant fear of a fall
or trust,
a trust that even if we go over the edge
we will be caught
in the arms of gracious Mystery.

A Saint

A third-grader got it right:
"A saint is someone that
the light shines through."

She was looking at a stained-glass window—
the one St. Francis inhabits.
Every morning the light comes
and St. Francis lets it pass through.

Saints are bearers of light
and love
and life.

Just ask any third-grader.

The Vine

"Lord Jesus, you are the true vine
and we are the branches: allow us to
 remain in you, to bear much fruit,
and to give glory to the Father."
  —*The Liturgy of the Hours,* vol. III, 967

The Vine spoke to me:
"Yes, I am the vine
and you participate in my life—
more, in my love and light.
My Father is the Ground of Being
in which I am rooted.
Our Holy Spirit is the sun and
the wind and the rain,
pouring forth the energy of grace.

And you and all others are branches,
existing because attached to me.
You share in everything I am and have—
most of all, in my friendship.
Through you I will bear fruit,
bringing peace, truth, charity, freedom, and justice
into the world,
filling everyone with compassion.

And when our friendship is deep and full,
glory will bursts forth with
the splendor of beauty,

the radiance of peace,
the ecstasy of joy.

Have no fear:
I am with, for, and in you."

O Danny Boy

Words have power,
but then add melody
and that power is multiplied.
Sung words stir the soul,
awaken memories,
foresee the future.
Tell me your songs,
I'll tell you who you are.

Even without words,
music is transformative.
How can one listen to Mozart
and remain the same?

Last night at the Memorial Mass
the lyrics of "O Danny Boy" were read,
with the melody silent in the air.
Tears flowed,
hands were held
We went home in sorrowful peace.

An Ode to Martha

"Martha, Martha,"
Jesus sighed.

That ancient struggle in every heart
between the duties of love
and the leisure of quiet seeing/being.
Mary sat; you worked.

But Jesus harbored a deep desire,
just to be with you—
beyond the joy of *being served*
into the happiness of *sheer presence.*

It was a unique moment,
a challenge to your ordinary path—
just to sit and be,
letting the dishes pile up,
dessert forgotten.

Tomorrow's duties would come.
For now, loving attention,
the only thing required.

Early-Night Music

She made music—
her instrument, a flute,
her place, the base of a bridge.

It was early evening,
when I passed by.
I dropped in a dollar
in gratitude for a slice of beauty
in an otherwise violent world.

For just the briefest of moments,
her lips left the flute to say "Thank you"
and then returned again
to continue the melody.

She made music.
She made a difference in my world.

Silence

Is silence the land
flowing with milk and honey?
Is it the promised land
where God dwells
and longs to speak to us?

Then why do we,
loquacious creatures,
fill our lives with ceaseless chatter,
with voices calling us to lands
devoid of ultimate meaning?

Be still, the great Book tells us,
and know that God is God.
Be silent,
awaiting in quiet expectancy,
calm trust,
gentle brooding,
a God who whispers His love
and fills the silence with His light.

Black Friday

The day after Thanksgiving,
but was it a good Friday
simply to avoid being in the red?
People interviewed on the nightly news:
"I didn't need it, but I bought it anyway."
"Shopping was as violent as last year."
"Wow! What a deal! Not sure what I will use it for."

Yes, at the end of the day—in the black.
Come Saturday, will it feel like a bad Friday,
the soul still insatiable
and weighed down by more stuff?

Friend-Maker

Can friends be made
or are intimate friendships sheer grace?

A man was hired.
Job description: make friends for the university.
His nickname: friend-maker.

I have met several matchmakers over the years.
Some of the marriages had fire,
some did not.
So much in life depends upon chemistry.

But a friend-maker!
The best one can do is introduce folks.
The rest altogether mystery.

A Question for Dame Julian

How could you live
without knowing the "what" and the "how"
of "that" great Trinitarian deed
by which all would be made well?

How deep your faith was!
How profound your trust in God's love.

Intercede for us, Dame Julian.
May we be granted your hazelnut grace
that it is divine Love holding all in being.

How could it be possible, therefore,
that all could be anything else than well?

Eulogies

On your mark,
　　get set,
　　　　go!

You have between five and ten minutes
　　to capture the essence of sixty, seventy,
　　eighty years of living.

Ten minutes to tell of
　　falling in love,
　　working forty-hour weeks,
　　celebrating countless holidays and weddings.

Don't forget the interior things:
　　the movement of the heart and soul,
　　the ministry of the memory and imagination.

Eulogists are given an impossible task
　　and yet, just today, I heard one verging on success.
A son spoke of his ninety-five-year-old father
　　in terms of endearment,
　　in words that painted an accurate portrait
　　of a life well spent.

The Lake

The lake was glass
and upon it was a canoe
in the morning mist.
I watched in silence from the shore.
Nothing moved,
not the wind,
not the water,
not even my soul.
I simply gazed
at the beauty of it all
If it was a portrait
it might be called
    "Peace"
        or
    "Morning Quiet"
        or
    "New Genesis."
The sun came around the corner,
from somewhere the wind arrived,
the canoe came to shore,
and the day began.

I Wish

I wish I could write
    a poem
        that was simple,
        as simple as a smile

    or one that ran smoothly,
        like the giant Mississippi
        or the quiet Nile

    and one that spoke directly
        and easily to the heart,
        like a confessor to a penitent.

But the wish is just a hope.

I keep looking over my shoulder
    at critics who don't even exist

    and struggle with doubts
        as to who cares
        or if words are ultimately futile.

So, like a self-conscious athlete,
    I stumble over my own feet,
        glancing at the scout and the crowd's approval.

~~I wish I could~~
write verse
like a morning lark singing to the dawn
in simple praise, in a hymn of joy.

Grace Mary Danison

Baptized, Dec. 27, 2006

Grace Mary,
   on the Feast of St. John the Evangelist,
   in the year of our Lord, 2006,
   at Resurrection Church in Allouez, Wisconsin,
   your dad held you over the baptismal font
   as the saving water of new life
   ran down your head in tears of joy.
Your mom held the baptismal candle
   while Ian, Alison, and Ben stood by in rapt attention.

Your baptism was on the same night
   that Grandpa John Manley celebrated eighty years of life.
Your baptism trumped his birthday,
   though the sixty guests came primarily for him.
But you were the star,
   brighter than the one that the Magi saw over Bethlehem.
You were a sign to us of life and love.
You filled the December darkness with a soft radiance,
   a gentle splendor
   completing our Christmas joy.

Dents

Dents,
scars,
warts
mark our days,
and irritate our hunger for perfection.

The scratch on the front right fender,
the healed wound on the index finger,
the blemishes on the south side of the soul—
all tell of life's imperfections.

Could these be, in the end,
badges of glory?
Would that we could
say "yes" to life's bruises.
Could they be God's will for you,
    for me?